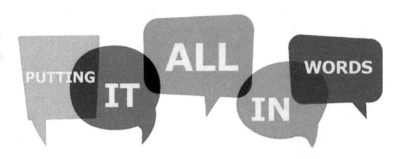

Y.L.G.U.
Young Lad God Understands

Putting It All In Words

HOV Publishing a division of HOV, LLC.
www.hovpub.com
hopeofvision@gmail.com

Cover Design: Hope of Vision Designs
Copy Editor: Clarity Communication
Editor/Proofread: Phyllis Miller-Bridges

Contact the Author, Tamara Martin at:
tamaraomara134@gmail.com

For further information regarding special discounts on bulk purchases, please visit www.hovpub.com

ISBN Paperback: 978-1-955107-99-0
ISBN eBook: 978-1-955107-98-3

10   9   8   7   6   5   4   3   2   1

Printed in the United States of America

Dedication

This book is dedicated to...

Those who have had to endure long-suffering;

Those who have been misunderstood;

Those who have ever been pinpointed, predicted, or categorized, but not of their own will;

Those who have been in the storm way too long;

Those who are hopeless romantics.

A word of inspiration to be remembered by all who read this: Although your light may be dim, know that it is still burning. With thanksgiving, I acknowledge the strength and support of my family. No matter how right, wrong, or indifferent; we are still family, and we will be, always and forever.

These books will be written in a series of three, which will have five chapters, to represent the Father, the Son and the Holy Ghost.

Special Thanks

To my sister, Francella, for being my biggest fan, and to Amy, who is not only my Sorority Sister, but my writing coach who helped to plant my creative seed.

Diana who also is an HOV Publishing author who has walked this journey prior to me. Thank you for your guidance on this journey.

Germaine Miller-Summers my publisher who not only believed in me, but that I could be healed through the writing process which had power to set me free.

Last, but not least, never to be forgotten is the one who paid it all for me— my Lord and Savior, Jesus Christ.

Epigraph

The takeaway is that of the old adage of we should not throw stones at glass houses. We now must realize the glass house is that of smoking mirrors and those who are throwing the stones are on the inside trying to break free. I freed myself…I was never stuck nor was I imprisoned because I found the importance within the power of Prayer.

Table of Contents

Chapter 1

Unknown Salvation ......……………………............. 1

Chapter 2

It's Me...Ugly ...……........……………...…........ 5

Chapter 3

Soul Seeking ……………………………........ 13

Chapter 4

Nothing Sacred ....………................. 19

Chapter 5

Folly Years ……………...................……........ 37

About the Author …………………….…............ 93

Putting It All In Words Notes …………….......... 95

Chapter 1

Unknown Salvation

I was one of the smallest preemies in the hospital. I only weighed three pounds. Three pounds is tiny! I had tiny lungs, tiny hands, tiny feet, and a tiny heart, yet there was something else wrong. I was diagnosed with Patent Ductus Arteriosus. It is a continuous opening between the two major blood vessels leading from the heart that normally closes shortly after birth, but mine never closed.

I was born into the glory of salvation that had been spoken over my life. My mother was and continues to be, a praying woman. Before I knew or could understand what salvation was, she prayed God's covering over me and pleaded with Him to keep me from dangers seen and unseen. I arrived two months early full of struggle. This was a preview of God's glory and His amazing grace. Tiny, with a compromised heart, I would need salvation. True salvation.

Medical salvation was the first priority. How do you preserve the life of a baby who weighs just three pounds and fits in the palm of her father's giant hand? How do you preserve the life of a baby born weighing just three pounds, and whose heart has an opening between the blood vessels leading from the heart? After staying in the hospital for two months, my first hope of salvation came when I was sent home. Yet, my heart was still not whole.

Countless doctor visits were leading me to another moment of salvation. When the day arrived, some five years later, something was different. Grandmother came to visit which is something that never occurred. The day was made even more special because Grandmother also presented me with a stuffed animal, a puppy that I named, Snoopy. Snoopy and I hopped into the car and arrived at the hospital. In my 5-year-old innocence, I walked into the hospital unaware that my medical salvation was at hand. Frequent doctor appointments were the norm for me. I didn't know that in just a little while, I'd be dressed head-to-toe in a hospital-issued gown, being prepped for surgery. I didn't know that Grandmother's visit was actually a prayer vigil. Her prayers and her faith moved the hand of God and thankfully, my salvation came to pass as my heart was repaired.

By God's grace and mercy, medical insurance through my father's job made it possible for me to receive the care that I needed. The prayers of my grandmother and mother, and the faith of my parents prepared the way for my medical healing and recovery. As my parents retold the story to me over the years, it was clear to me that they knew that no man— specifically, no doctor— would have the final say over their baby. I realize now that I learned how to pray from my mother.

Although my earliest years were a journey through a maze of doctor appointments, challenges, and surgery, I was left with no limitations. I emerged as a young healthy child who could run, jump, and play just like my friends. Nothing held me back physically, yet the struggle to full salvation and complete healing was just beginning.

I was taught to treat others the way that I wanted to be treated. Although I was born with an imperfect heart, it's capacity to care for others was abundant. Growing up, I could see no color, I could see no race, and I could see no creed. Perhaps, knowing the fragility of life at such a young age formed my character in an extraordinary way. Perhaps I could see differently and love differently than other children. In my innocence, I sincerely treated others the way that I wanted to be treated. I was so full of innocence and love, but as I got older, the love was replaced by loneliness and hurt. It turned ugly, and Ugly was my name.

Chapter 2

It's Me... Ugly

My earliest school memories were pure. I had honest friends that I had grown to know from my neighborhood. We attended the same daycare as toddlers, then we moved on to the same religious elementary school. In my neighborhood, it was normal for parents to send their children to Holy Trinity Catholic School. My parents wanted me and my brother to have a better education than they had, and Holy Trinity was one of the best. I remain thankful for that foundation. It taught me things that I continue to hold dear in life— religion, free will and choices, morals, and values. I also learned some other things that have remained with me like discipline, penalties, and the reality of hell.

As I entered elementary school, the rules set by my father weighed me down. I was always told that he did not want any problems and that he did not raise his kids to be in trouble! I knew that I better not be a problem child at school. The consequence of being dealt with at home was enough to keep me in line. I desperately tried to stay under my big brother's wing, but we would butt heads from time to time. I wanted his attention, but my nagging often got on his nerves. He was seven years older than me, so even when I wasn't getting on his nerves, there was not much that he could do to protect me when I needed him. During the years that we were in school together, our classrooms were on different floors. I learned to survive without the covering of my brother.

The faces that I saw in class were familiar. Some were neighborhood friends, some I knew from daycare, and some I fellowshipped with at my church. Yet something started to happen, and I was reminded of my name, Ugly. My innocence was met by cruelty. My dark skin was not like my classmates. While the teacher was teaching colors, I learned from my classmates that my color was not considered as pretty as other children. As the teacher taught length and measurements, I learned from my classmates that my hair was short, in comparison to others. Again, I learned that what others thought of me meant that my name, Ugly, suited me.

My parents had an expectation that by enrolling me in a Catholic school, I would not only learn and get smarter, but that I would not be torn down. Unfortunately for me, their expectations were not met. I learned how to accept being teased. I learned to add the scars and trauma of school to those scars that remained from my heart surgery. Afterall, I am Ugly. Of course, I should accept that my journey would leave me bruised with deep cuts and scars that would need to be healed.

By the time middle school began, I was the target of everyone's jokes. Being treated rudely and being hurt by classmates who were supposed to be my friends made me question the salvation that I'd felt surrounding me earlier in life. My fear of being labeled a snitch or a troublemaker made me keep quiet. I remained committed to the earliest lesson that I had learned at home, which was to treat other people the way that I wanted to be treated. For some reason, not getting them in trouble was more important than speaking up for myself. Afterall, I was Ugly and somehow, being treated that way seemed appropriate.

One day, Copper Willow, a girl from my class, sat down next to me at the lunch table. I couldn't believe that she was sitting next to me... Ugly! My heart tumbled. Maybe I wasn't so ugly after all, maybe she wanted to be my friend. With a quickness, I was flooded with hope as I imagined having playdates on the weekends, having a friend to jump rope with, and maybe even someone to actually call my best friend. I was so tired of being left out of everything unless I was being cast as the boy in the childhood game of playing house. My joy was short-lived as her hands quickly moved beneath the lunch table, traveling across my lap until they were under my skirt. Is this what friends do? I wondered as she felt between my legs. She was moving as if this was what she was supposed to be doing to me, so I didn't protest. I didn't yell and I didn't stop her. It became "our thing." Sometimes she had a chance in the bathroom, or in the library. She would feel on me whenever she had an opportunity to be alone with me. Again, I didn't protest, I didn't yell and I didn't stop her. I did just what she told me, which was to keep it a secret. She said that if I told anyone, she would deny it, beat me up, and say that I was the one who did those things to her. By her threat alone, not only did I know what she was doing was wrong, but Copper Willow obviously knew it was wrong too.

Even though it felt wrong, I'd never been told or taught that it was wrong. The conversation about good and bad touches is shared in a lot of homes, but my home was not one of them. There are a lot of families where parents talk openly with their children about not letting anyone (not a friend, an uncle, an aunt, a pastor, a babysitter, a teacher, a coach, etc.) touch them in their bathing suit areas. My family was not one of those families.

Even back then, I thought about the ugliness of it all. I started to wonder, What's wrong with me? Why is this happening? Was I supposed to be born a boy? Maybe if I were born a boy, this wouldn't be happening. I could not understand, but somehow, it was easier to just be the boy. Every time we played house, I was told that I was the man, and I willingly went along with it. I never stuck up for myself, but I realize now that I was just like my mother. At home, she never stuck up for herself; it was easier that way. I had short hair and accepted the role that the kids gave me. I quietly played along. I was told that I looked like a boy. And since I looked like a boy, I was expected to act like the man in all of these childhood games of playing house. I had to touch and be touched... I had to kiss and be kissed. I was doing what was expected of me just to be included in the games and to not be picked on. Being the man and fitting into how other kids saw me and who I was expected to be had become the norm. I just went along with being the man or acting like the husband.

One day, I played house with my neighbor, Lia Fence, while our older brothers were left in charge of us. There we were, two little girls on a playdate! I was excited! Instead of me and Lia playing with dolls or watching television, Lia suggested that we snoop through my father's closet. We quickly came across videotapes and snuck them into my room. Like most children, we were excellent at imitating what we saw.

Those movies, hidden for a reason, gave us a new game to play. We did what they did. Imitating what we saw, I put my mouth on her body in ways that I had no business doing. As an adult, it's now easy to say that we were children who were innocently playing and that neither of us thought that we were doing anything wrong. Yet, we knew enough to sneak... We knew enough to hide our new game behind the closet door in my room. I was not exposed to sex in my household like the other little girls I played with. I knew that it was wrong because of how our older siblings reacted when they caught us. My brother told me that I was nasty and not to do it again or he would tell our mother. I cried and begged him not to tell. Even though I didn't know why what I had done was wrong, I was scared of what my mother would do.

Although my brother never tattled on me, he made sure that the fear of being found out hung over my head. He blackmailed me. Later in life, I would learn that lying and how to be deceitful were things that he'd learned from our father. Whenever he wanted me to do something, like his chores or to get away from him when his friends were over, all he would say was "If you don't do it, I will tell mommy about it." That was my cue to do whatever was asked of me. I was blackmailed by my own brother. Instead of helping me, my brother was unintentionally traumatizing me in ways that I would only understand in my adult years. I had a pit in my stomach, but I never uttered one word.

Chapter 3
Soul Seeking

You would think that after years of being teased and bullied in elementary school, I would have developed a thick skin. You would think that maybe I would have gotten used to the name calling and the teasing. Or maybe that I would have developed some method of coping by going to my older brother for protection, or at the very least, for advice. But he was going through his own struggle and his survival skills did not necessarily include looking out for me. So, at a young age, I had picked up enough spiritual knowledge to know that I could go to the Lord in prayer. I knew that God was around and available to me every day of the week. Each night as I laid my head down on my pillow, I would just pray for the next day to be a better day than the one that I'd just lived through.

An answer to my prayers for better days would have meant that my parents' issues would have disappeared. I was concerned about them. Their issues kept me from confiding in them about my own issues. Although it was normal for me to hear them yelling and screaming, and to witness the slaps, punches, and abuse that no child should witness, I wanted to protect my parents from having to worry about me. In my young mind, I thought it would be inappropriate to add to what already seemed to be large problems between them.

With an eerie predictability, after every fight my mother would say to me, "Your daddy loves you. It will be okay... Mommy is okay and I'm sorry." I think back on this consistent declaration of acceptance and still feel the confusion that I felt at the time. Why would Mommy apologize when she's the one bloodied and in tears? What was she sorry for?

My Daddy, the man who always brought her to this state of shameful humiliation in front of her children, is a perfect character study of the struggle of humans to be more like Christ, yet imperfect in so many ways. I have lost count of the number of times Daddy has stood up in church to share his testimony about meeting my mother.

It was a Sunday morning during testimony time, and he was tarrying before the Lord, pouring out his heart at the altar. When he finally came to himself and opened his eyes, there she stood, his bride-to-be, his future wife, my mother.

This is what I could not wrap my head around. Daddy, why not tell the full story? Why not share the testimony that the Lord blessed you with my mother, yet you periodically forget about the goodness of the Lord, and you go upside her head as if you were doing the work of Satan himself? Why not tell it all? At least then maybe deliverance could come for all of us after the confession. Maybe then that ugliness could have been prayed out of him or prayed off him. But no, instead, he passed the ugliness down to me. Although, it looks different and I don't beat on anyone, I am Ugly, just the same.

The merry-go-round of beatings went on more often than I even like to admit to myself, but after every fight she delivered the same "Your Daddy Loves You" speech, which concluded with her apology. If Daddy was a monster, then my older brother was my personal He Man. I would stick to him like glue, hoping that through him I could escape any version of the love that my mother described my father having for me. Our bond was unbreakable. We often played our own version of "Wonder Woman." He nicknamed me "Escaper" because after tying me up and outfitting me in zipped-up backwards jackets, I would twist and wiggle out of any binding that he made for me. I was so tiny that no Boy Scout knots he tied around me could hold me for very long. I wonder now, if there was a lesson meant for me in learning how to escape. Was it that in spite of being tied into what seemed like a helpless or hopeless situation, I wasn't stuck, I wasn't imprisoned? I wonder why no one ever taught my mother how to escape?

Watching her escape would have been better than hearing her cry. One time her cries were so loud and the sounds of slapping and punching seemed like they would never stop. My brother would tell me to stay in his room. This command had become common, I knew what it meant. As I watched him place his tennis shoes near the door ever so quietly and carefully ahead of time, I knew that he was going in. Like a superhero ready for a showdown, he'd run into my parents' room and pull my father off of my mother, declaring, "Okay Dad, she's had enough! Enough!" Shielding our mother from him, my brother would stand in front of our father. Just like that, it would be over, and the final words would be an apology uttered by my mother. "I'm sorry, not in front of the kids." Even in my young mind, I knew that this phrase made no sense. Not in front of the kids! So, if it weren't done in front of us, would it be okay for him to beat her? I never understood how after all the drama and ugliness of the night before, my mother would be up early the next morning performing all her wifely duties. The bed would be made and a beautiful home-cooked breakfast would be set in front of my father as if he was deserving of this type of devotion and love. My mother so perfectly placed a mask on her face to cover all the ugliness that was going on. The mask covered the bruises, her broken heart, her disappointments, and her shattered dreams. I learned from the best. The mask made everything possible and my mother's mask taught me that the better you can mask your pain, the better you are as a woman, wife, mother, and even Christian. Masks make it possible to believe that it's more important to be what someone else needs you to be (a secret keeper, a punching bag, a sex slave, a servant), rather than what you need for yourself to be (strong, confident, demanding of sincere love, etc.).

Chapter 4
Nothing Sacred

I had so much to keep to myself and I hoped that I would catch a break somewhere but that was far from happening. I received abuse at school five days a week. At home, my mother was unhappy, my father acted in ways that I did not like, and my brother was lost in his own thoughts. I knew that I could only go to God. Even my place of worship, my church home where I used to be able to find peace, became Hell after a new Pastor was appointed to lead the church. The size of his family was shocking, with enough kids to form a basketball team. They were yet another group that would begin picking on me just like the kids in school.

Just like that, I was getting battered at school and at church, seven days a week. I learned to wear a mask so that no one could see the pain upon me. I vowed to never let anyone know. In Sunday School, the preacher's kids, better known as the "PKs," particularly the boys, would be so cruel to me. They would draw horrible pictures of things and put my name on them. One of the pictures they would draw was called "The Fly." I didn't look like my classmates or the friends I interacted with on a daily basis. I didn't have light skin, I was brown-skinned. I was very skinny and had very little meat on my bones. I had no shape at all and unlike other little girls who needed to wear training bras, I was the complete opposite. I was wearing undershirts and looked exactly like my older brother. I wore big bright red glasses and I had not grown into my womanhood early like my friends.

Based on the parables that I had learned at Catholic School, I accepted that I was created differently according to God's design, not that I really understood why. However, it was a soft quiet confirmation for me. As I underwent the taunting of being called the Fly, along with the sound effects and the silly jokes that made others laugh; the tears would come to my eyes, but I never allowed them to see me break. I never allowed them to see me cry. I always held it in until I could go to a corner or a bathroom stall, and cry ever so quietly by myself. Once, I cried in the church basement at Vacation Bible School because one of the preacher's sons, Miquel, poured glitter in my hair. My friend Vicki and the Vacation Bible School teacher saw what happened and tried their best to comfort me. I wore a Jheri Curl and even though I was not supposed to get my hair wet, I excused myself from the arts and crafts table and stuck my head in the sink to wash it out.

I was in tears knowing my mother would snap because she had spent her hard-earned money on my hair appointment. Now, that money was wasted because the water would cause my Jheri Curl to get completely dried out. Not only could I not tell my mom what happened and why, but I had to lie to her about it even though my mother's main rule was to always tell the truth. I told her that I'd allowed my friends to squirt me with a water gun. Instead of those who deserved it, I took all the blame and all of the punishment. Luckily, my mother's stylist thought the chemicals did not take and she redid my hair for free.

This was one of the many times that the PKs took things too far, one of the Sunday School teachers noticed the way that I was withdrawing. I was not open and talkative like I used to be, so she called my mother to express her concern for me. The phone call made my mother aware of what was going on. Once, we were in church, she saw a drawing that one of the preacher's sons, Jonathan, had made of a nasty-looking fly with my name on it. She saw the hurt on my face and called the pastor's wife to see why her kids were picking on me.

The preacher was a kind and gentle man and my mother felt comfortable calling his wife to see if she could resolve the issue with her children picking on me. Surprisingly, the preacher's wife, known as The First Lady, was the opposite of her husband. She was not warm and gracious, and she was not sensitive and caring. When my mother expressed her concerns, The First Lady denied that her children were involved in mistreating me because she didn't like no junk and she didn't like no mess.

Although, this was not what my mother wanted to hear and it was not how she expected The First Lady to respond, out of respect for the pastor she did not go in on his wife. Afterwards, my mother and I talked about what I had overheard from their phone conversation. In spite of The First Lady's tone and her smug attitude, my mother vowed to protect me. However, I didn't want to be in a church where I needed to be protected and I didn't want to stay there. I decided to leave my home church, the place where I had been baptized and raised. I just wanted the pain to go away.

My mother was peeved, she was so upset that she told everyone that the preacher's kids needed to go, not me. This was a battle she would never win because it would require taking the whole case to the Bishop's level. So, instead of calling people out and being called a snitch or a cry baby, I left. My mother was so upset about the situation that she talked about the matter with members of the church and her friends as well. Eventually, one of her coworkers suggested that my mother take me to her church. She stated that not only were there a lot of kids at her church, but as the choir director she would love to have me.

Even though this new church was a different denomination, I was able to adapt. Going to a school that was a different denomination than my church had helped me to be comfortable no matter the style of worship. As I attended the new church, I started to come out of the shell that I had put myself in. I love to sing, especially in church. It makes me feel really connected and like I cannot go wrong when it comes to Him. I felt as if I would come into my own skin when singing of the Lord, instead of being pushed in the corner and silenced like when I was in my old church. Here, I was free and able to spread my wings. In this house of God everyone was seen and appreciated equally. I was able to show my love for the Lord in my own special way. I was not born with the gift of singing really well, nor did I play an instrument. My gift was a gift of prayer and if I meditated and went to God, He would fill my spirit and create something beautiful. I got my peace back with no distractions at church. I was able to handle the things at home and in school that I was carrying through life on an everyday basis.

Well, my light may have been dim, but it still was burning. The light was beneath my feet and guided my way. I finally had a church home where I felt comfortable, but things at school and at home were not getting any better. Since I was getting older, I began to understand more about why my parents were not getting along. My father was an unfaithful husband.

In my family, my father believed that his role was to provide for his family by keeping a roof over our heads and making sure that we had everything that we needed. As long as he did that, he thought that he should be able to go out and drink and hang out to unwind without my mother giving him any lip. He expected my mother to keep her mouth shut about his behavior, stay home, raise the children, and keep up with her wifely duties. My mother held up her end and she never let my father's lifestyle affect the well-being of the household or her children and our education. If that were to happen, a greater level of hell would run through the home.

My mother continually expressed that she wanted my father to respect her, he always used the home that he'd provided, as evidence that she was respected. He believed because we had a roof over our heads and food to eat, that my mother should feel respected. What he could not see was that the respect she actually wanted could never be felt through the material things that he could give her. Instead, she wanted an equal partnership in their union. Even though that's what she needed, due to his upbringing, my father would never see my mother on the same level as himself. My mother yearned for respect so deeply and at times she would fight for it. However, it was a battle that she knew when to pick and choose. So, when my father's unfaithful ways started to seep into the lives of me and my older sibling, life got worse. In addition to how my parents would fight, life was worse for me at school as well.

My father knew that he had a great family, and he was never going to leave his wife or walk away from his children. When a woman that he had been seeing wanted him to do so, he told her that he didn't want her *like that.* The woman acted so badly that she pretended to be my mother and called my school stating that she'd be there to pick me up early for a doctor's appointment. As I sat in the office for an entire class period waiting to be picked up, the school finally called my mother to let her know that I had been waiting for her. Then, the truth unfolded that *she* had never called the school and that there was never an appointment. Even though this led to more fighting between my parents, I still was not grasping what my father was doing to my mother. A student at my school made sure that I would understand soon enough.

One fateful day, my classmate Hillary overheard a girl named Aleza say that *my* father was with a member of her family. Instead of telling me directly, Aleza went around school telling everyone except me, which is how my friend found out. This was the first time that my parents' problems, specifically my father's infidelity, became clear to me.

I had an out-of-body experience. After hearing the news, I was zoned out and went through the motions of going to each class, but I didn't speak to anyone. How dare she repeat my family's business? I was furious and numb at the same time! In my family, children were always taught to stay in a child's place. We never repeated grown folks' business. We never spoke out of turn and even if we knew their business, we never repeated anything.

Finally, when I went to the cafeteria to eat lunch, I saw Aleza. As I walked past the dessert cart, I picked the whole thing up and swung it with all of my might, hitting her in the stomach. Without uttering a word, I calmly walked myself to the principal's office. I was not a frequent visitor to the principal's office because I'd always obeyed my father's rule to not be a problem child. The teachers and the principal knew what I had done was out of character for me and they called my mother immediately. Unfortunately, they called Aleza's mother as well and when her mother arrived at the school, she started yelling at me. All she knew was what I had done to her child; she was not aware of what her child had done to me. The woman yelled at me so loudly that my mother, who was being debriefed in another room, could hear her and came to my defense. My mother told her that instead of addressing me, she needed to be speaking to her own child to teach her to stop repeating grown folks' business and then she politely informed her of what Aleza had done. The girl's mother then went to the nurse's office and held nothing back in the presence of the administration, unlike my mother. My mother knew that her battle was not with them, but with my father.

Luckily, I was not expelled from school for this incident. After speaking with me, the principal could see that I was not in my right mind. I was actually offered counseling if I wanted to talk to someone. Once we were home, my mother asked me how I really felt, but I refused to open up. I just told her that the thing that I was most upset about was that the girl didn't just come to me directly, but that she had embarrassed me by telling our family's business and made me the laughingstock of the school. That is why I had to deal with her the way that I did. Nothing more came of it.

I struggled to keep my focus in school because there was another issue that I had to face. I wasn't grasping the material well enough to reach my full potential. Instead of As and Bs, I was bringing home Cs and Ds. I had to seek help from a tutor, as well as one of my teachers. When I got the help that I needed to be successful, not only did the teachers know that I could do the work, but it was a positive distraction from everything negative in my life. I developed a small tick in my shoulders; whenever the teasing would start, my shoulder would jump. I had a great sense of humor and used it to my advantage by using it as a distraction. I often fell down the stairs or out of my chair to get the kids to laugh *with* me and not *at* me. My plan was somewhat successful because when the kids saw how funny I was, some of them stopped being mean. Unfortunately, this coping mechanism only worked with the Caucasian students. The African American students didn't care, they remained cruel beyond measure.

This was a private school, and every so often kids would leave and return to public school due to financial concerns. Good thing for me, those students who were mean and cruel were the ones who left and returned to public school. My parents were blessed with good jobs and great benefits. They wanted their children to do even better than they had, so they gave us unlimited access to education, which they believed would take us far. Anytime I fell below the bar, help was always offered to get me back on track and make sure that I could be successful with my academics.

Although the teasing had lessened at school, things were not improving at home. I could never have it both ways. By this time, my older brother had gone on to college and at home I had taken on the role of being the protector of our mother, just as he had shown me how to do. As arguments would flare up, I would stay up on guard, listening to the *grown folks* and making sure that things didn't go too far. This one night would be remembered by the entire household forever.

On this particular day, I was supposed to go out to eat with both of my parents, but once again my father stayed out drinking in the bars and did not come home. So, my mother took me to get something from a fast-food restaurant. Afterwards, she bathed me and put me to bed. When she thought I was asleep, my mother left the house to confront my father at the bar. One thing led to another and after fussing in the streets they came home. They entered the house yelling and screaming so loudly that I was up and alert. After going downstairs, I sat listening as my parents continued to argue in the kitchen. I overheard my mother tell him to leave her alone so that she could take her medication. The fighting had gotten so bad that my mother had started taking medication to handle the depression she was feeling.

I knew that my mother had taken her medicine, but my father kept on antagonizing her. He never knew how to let stuff go; he was of the mindset that things were over when *he said* they were over. When he came into the living room and saw me sitting there, he yelled at me to go to bed. I ran up to the top of the stairs and sat in the darkness where I couldn't be seen. As I listened, it seemed like their argument would never end, but suddenly my mother came around the corner and as she peeked through the darkness, she saw me. After she hurried me to bed, repeating what my father had already told me to do, I went to my brother's room and listened as the chaos continued.

Finally, I heard my mother tell my father to shut up because he was working her nerves and she had to take her medicine. I knew that she had already taken it and though I wanted to say something, I was so scared that I didn't have the courage to tell her not to take her pills. I didn't know that I could have prevented harm from coming to her had I mustered enough courage to run down the stairs to prevent her from taking a second dose.

When the next morning came, I woke up and ran to my parents' room, but this day was different. As I looked around, the bed was not made, but my mother's shoes and purse were in their normal place. I ran down the stairs and into the kitchen. There was no smell of breakfast, nor were any sandwiches being made. Instead, my father sat at the table with tears in his eyes and speechless. I cried out for my mother repeatedly, but she did not answer. What had he done to my mother?

My father explained that my mother did not wake up that morning, so he took her to the hospital. Immediately, I cried out and begged my father to call my brother, but he refused. He was taking his finals and my father insisted that this news could not be shared with him while he was testing. It would have to wait until afterwards. I was too young to visit my mother in the ICU, I had to stay with her parents and send my love through them. My grandfather was my world. I was his *"Sweet Cake"* and he was my *"Tay Tay."* Even though we had no blood relation, because he and my grandmother adopted my mother, he loved my mother and her children as if they were blood.

My grandfather would keep me in the church as much as possible to distract me from the fact that my mother was in a coma from a drug overdose. It was hard on me, but it was even harder on my brother when he came home. He couldn't understand why no one called him. His mother was far more important to him than his finals.

Our grandparents tried to be there for us as much as possible. At that time, more than ever, I needed to hear that I was loved and that I was beautiful. I needed positivity spoken into my life. Although I received it from my grandfather, I never heard that from my father. Even though I would often be told, "You know your daddy loves you." He never told me directly. I never received any sort of affection from him like that of my grandfather. He never skipped a beat though. He always let us know how much he loved us. He played with me constantly and would get me any animal my heart desired. Whether I wanted a goldfish, a bird, a cat, or a rabbit, nothing was off limits. He even took me fishing and this time with him was priceless. He would try his best to shine light on the family during our darkest hours, but even more so now. We had to be strong and pull together.

God was in everything that happened that night and for the next couple of days. All of this occurred during the Thanksgiving season, it was the first Thanksgiving without my mother. She was the one who always cooked awesome meals. This

Thanksgiving, the meal was nowhere near what our family would have had if my mother was the one who prepared it.

It took a few weeks but eventually my mother returned home. She vowed never to leave her children again. When I asked her what had happened, my mother replied that she did something stupid, but God made her realize that it was not her time and that her children needed her. She told me that she wasn't going anywhere and that no one and nothing would keep her from her family.

After all the ugliness, my father sat down and vowed his love for my mother. He promised that he would never lay another hand on her again. He confessed that he could not see himself without her, and that he didn't know that things were so bad that she wanted to leave him. Slowly, he began to understand that his fists were damaging and not necessary in order to get his point across. Little by little, we were becoming the family that I'd hoped for.

Chapter 5
Folly Years

No matter how mean and cruel the jokes were about my mother, I pressed forward and never let anyone see me break. I had developed a thick skin to get me through all of the torment I faced at school. I endured hell at school, as well as at my new place of worship.

I had been terrorized by other "PKs" from my old church home, but here, there were only two, so I decided to stop running and deal with it. I graduated from the private school with the help from counselors, tutors, and teachers, which was great, but that meant that I would be moving on to a new public school for high school.

I knew that I would have to face some of the kids from my old school and thought if I could get-in good with them, I would be able to avoid the hazing process that I'd heard about.

On the first day of school, I learned that I was wrong. As I waited outside to enter the building, I encountered a girl named Charity who was triple my size. Charity sat on me to get a laugh from the other kids just because I was small and skinny. The laughter from this group of kids cut deeper than the abuse that I'd become accustomed to. The class size was double what it had been in my old school, and this abuse was physical versus the verbal abuse I was used to. I knew from that day forward that the next four years would be packed with more hell than I could imagine. With the situations that I'd gone through at home, the door was not open for me to go to my mother. There was still abuse in my home. The physical abuse may have stopped, but the verbal abuse continued, and the words hurt worse than a slap or even a bloody nose. Even as a young teen I knew that wasn't right, still it seemed that no one in my life had the power to make abuse stop. So, again my only outlet was to pray and cry out to God.

My house was only a few blocks away from the high school, so after school I would run all the way home, or at least far enough away where I knew the other kids would not follow me. I was picked on for being the person that my parents were raising me to be. They did not want me to fit into the stereotypes of black culture. I could not wear the clothes that would make me fit in. Instead of looking like one of the girls in an R&B or rap video, I was dressed in preppy clothes. Because of this, I didn't fit in with any of the black kids that I went to school with, and they punished me for it. My father grew up dirt poor in the south, one of eleven kids in his family; he wore hand-me-down clothes. Both of my parents wanted to make sure that we fit into *American* culture, rather than *Black* culture. American culture, so they said, was the one that we'd need to fit into to land a job and be successful.

My family didn't live in the same neighborhood as most of the black families, or in the projects, so the kids at school hated me. We lived in a predominantly white neighborhood. The black kids assumed that I thought I was better than everyone else because I'd gone to a private school. I was abused because of my parents' decisions to give me certain opportunities and experiences. It was a hefty price to pay for something that wasn't my fault. Running from kids who made my life miserable was something that I had to suffer through every day. As I ran with tears in my eyes, I prayed to not be hurt or beaten up too badly so that I wouldn't have to lie to my mother about marks or bruises. Little did I know, even if no one could physically see bruises on the outside, each experience scarred me deeply on the inside. I would get out of school every day at 2:45 pm and cry about my day. By the time my mother arrived home from work at 3:15 pm, I would have cleaned myself up, wiped my tears, and be seated at the table doing my homework. When my mother asked how my day was, I'd answer, "It was fine." On days when my father was not working a double shift, or triple overtime, he would come home at 3:30 pm and ask the same question about my day. To him I'd reply with the same answer, "My day was fine."

My looks still had not matured like the other females in my class. My hair was no longer that it had been, I still had to wear glasses, and although my baby teeth were gone, crooked teeth were now in their place. I was called names like Black Olive Oil, Jabber Jaws, Four Eyes, and Celie from "The Color Purple" by Alice Walker. As if that wasn't bad enough, I was not allowed to have a boyfriend, or even to give my number out to boys so that they could call my house. The kids started to say that I must like girls instead of boys, and that I was *funny*.

The kids found out quickly that I was not a troublemaker and that I would not be the one to start, or even finish a fight. They would pluck me in the head during class when the teachers would not notice, yet if they did notice, they did not say anything. Lunchtime was the worst because the teachers ate lunch in a separate room from us. We were not monitored, so the kids would slap me in the head with lunch trays. Actually, all of the unmonitored areas of the school were horrible. I was tripped in the hallway and pushed into the lockers. In the locker room, kids would turn on the shower and push me in. I would not fight back; not because I was afraid of them, but because I was afraid of my father. Getting in trouble at school meant getting in even more trouble at home.

Up until this point, I had a good reputation with my teachers and my guidance counselor. My guidance counselor was a member of my home church and had known me since I was born. The faculty and staff knew that I was not someone who they saw in the office over and over again. I was not in detention or suspended for bad behavior, but my good track record was about to change. That year for Christmas I received a ring-watch from my mother. During this era wearing rings was kind of a big deal, and it was an even bigger deal when you wore rings on every finger like I did.

One day while in English class, I took my rings off as I sat at my desk putting lotion on my hands. As I put my rings back on, I realized one was missing. Within the blink of an eye, *the ring* was gone. I looked on the floor and all over the classroom but did not find it. I was so upset just thinking about what my mother would do because I could not keep up with my jewelry. I asked the entire class who had taken my ring. Little did I know, the class thought it would be funny to lie and say that Monie, the meanest girl in the school had taken it. This led to a fight! Unaware of being set up, I fell for the prank. I went to Monie and demanded my ring back. She told me that it was best for me to get out of her face because she didn't take my ring. However, because the rest of the class kept telling me that they saw Monie take it, they pushed me into not backing down. I felt especially confident since one of the kids in my class, Dana, went to my church. Dana was known for being tough, and I assumed that she would have my back, that nothing too bad would happen to me.

I confronted Monie and told her, "You better give me back my ring, or else!" Monie stood up and told me that it was going to be on after the bell rang. I was petrified! I went to Dana and asked her if she had my back for the fight that I had to face up to after school.

"Nope!" she said as she laughed in my face. "We just want to see a fight, and that fight doesn't have anything to do with me." I pleaded with her, "But she's bigger than me. What am I going to do?" You better hit her first. That's all I can tell you!

The anxiety had gotten the best of me and even when the bell rang and Monie walked out of the class, I followed her and instigated the confrontation all on my own. With my big mouth, I yelled out, "Yo, Monie! Where are you going? The bell rang! What's up? Are you scared?"

Monie dropped her books, turned around, and made her way back to me. I heard the kids say, "What are you doing? She was going to let you go! You're in for it now!"

It was too late to back-out now, and before I knew it, Monie was in my face. I two-pieced her with a left and a right. The kids went wild! I only weighed in at a buck-o-five soaking wet, so Monie scooped me up and body-slammed me. She put her foot on my chest and stomped on me as I lay on the floor. Finally, the teachers came and broke it up, which led to more pandemonium. You see, in my school if you helped a teacher to break up a fight, you could get a pass to leave campus and go to the Hardee's across the street to eat lunch. So, when the teacher announced that she needed two volunteers to escort us to the office, the kids went wild fighting over who would take us. During the tugging back and forth, someone scratched me in the face. The only mark that I had from the actual fight was a size 10 shoe print on my shirt from the other girl.

As we waited in the Principal's Office, the girl turned to me and said, "I hope you know I didn't steal your ring. The girl who was sitting behind you did, but they lied to you so that we'd fight. I wasn't even going to fight you until you opened your mouth. I have to give you credit though, you stood up to me, so we're cool. I may be mean, but only to those who deserve it. That's why I never bother you."

The principal came in and said how disappointed he was in my behavior. I was suspended for 10 days. On the first day, I was to stay home to think about what I did. Since I'd never been in trouble before, for the nine remaining days, I had to report to school for my in-school suspension. Since the other girl stayed in trouble, she received a 10-day out-of-school suspension. I tried to tell our principal that Monie and I had made up and that it would never happen again, but he did not listen to anything that I had to say. When the phone call was made to my house, my father answered and was told to come to the school to pick me up.

The ride home was unbearable. I tried to explain what had happened so that he would understand, but it didn't matter to him. Once we were home, he continued to yell at me so loudly that the neighbors could hear him. When my mother pulled up into the driveway, she could hear him from outside. When my mother asked what was going on, he demanded that I tell her.

After I explained everything to her, my mother gently told me to go to my room since my father had punished me enough by yelling. As I walked up the stairs to change my clothes, get cleaned up, and get ready for supper, I heard my mother coming to my defense by asking my father what was wrong with him. She didn't want me to be anybody's doormat, and even though they did not tolerate fighting, my father should have praised me because I had finally stood up for myself. He should have been proud of me.

After staying home for the first day of the suspension, I returned to school for the in-school suspension, and I loved it! It was actually great to be in the room with no talking, no one picking on me, no teasing, and nothing to distract me from my lesson. When I returned to my regular classroom, some of the kids actually stopped bothering me, while some of the relentlessly cruel kids, the ones with no home training, just pushed more to try to get me to my breaking point. No matter what, I still never let them see me cry.

As freshman year came to an end and I moved onward to my sophomore year, there were still some things that my parents did not allow. Namely, the rule set by my father that I was not allowed to date. However, I was a normal teenage girl, I loved the boys that I knew I couldn't talk to. Ones who were popular, like the star football, volleyball, and basketball players, were my weakness. They never even noticed how I would look at them at lunch or when they passed my locker in the hallway. However, some of the girls in my classes noticed, and they used that against me to embarrass me in front of the boys. They knew that I was shy and that I didn't even know how to speak to a boy. They would put me on the spot by convincing the hottest guy to speak to me; then laugh when my voice would close up and the word hello couldn't even leave my lips. They'd joke on me saying that I looked stupid or that I must be a mute since I couldn't speak. I'd then become the center of attention as Melanie Marriott, one of the popular girls, would say, "You don't want her, you want someone like me."

They were so mean that they had Martin Heartman, one of the hottest boys in school, tell me that he would have sex with me and break my back like the pencil in his hand. He then broke the pencil in two. I was so upset that I ran away from them literally thinking that the pencil was me; it was as if he had really broken me. Since no one ever sat down and told me about the birds and the bees, I didn't know what to think.

One thing that I'd noticed was how people treated you if you were a star athlete. In an effort to not be picked on, I decided to try out for sports. It was hard since I didn't come from a family that was naturally athletic like some of the kids. Some of these kids were legacies; their parents, or brothers and sisters had come before them and laid the path for them to play. My older brother played football, but he wasn't a star athlete either. Even though I wasn't naturally athletic, the one thing I did have was height. I was tall and skinny and the coaches liked that when it came to track, basketball, and dance. I stuck at it, but because I wasn't the fastest or one of the starting players, I still got teased for that. The teasing only made me want to be better and do better, so I stayed with it. It even got my father to come see me play. I was hopeful that this would be a way for us to bond, but no matter what I did, it wasn't good enough for him either. My mother didn't want me to appear like too much of a tomboy, so she pushed me into dance.

The Homecoming Dance was coming up and my mother set me up on a date with Alvin Grace. Our mothers knew each other, and they made it happen. Since Alvin was younger than me, he didn't really know about the name calling and he saw me for who I was. Having him as my date made me feel good until the kids at the dance noticed us. They knew Alvin from the neighborhood, so they went easy on him, but behind his back they ridiculed me. They said that he was my date because he felt sorry for me, and that his mother must have made him be my date because I was too ugly for someone to take seriously. After noticing my mood change, he asked if I was okay. In spite of being devastated, I told Alvin that I was fine, I even told him that if he didn't want to dance with me, he could hang with the kids from the neighborhood and I'd understand. He stayed with me and tried to cheer me up, but the damage was already done.

Although the cruel jokes never lost their sting, I did my best to cope and tried not to let it faze me anymore. I was tired of it, and it seemed to me that the kids should have grown tired of picking on me as well. Yet, instead of them thinking, *Oh well, let's leave her alone*, they took it up a notch.

One day the kids said they would be nice to me for two days straight to earn my trust. Little did I know that it was just so that they could pull off a prank that one of my classmates came up with. They planned to tell me that they bought some grease that would help my hair grow since I still had short hair and most of the girls wore ponytails. In actuality, it wasn't grease, it was the therapeutic cream that the trainers would use when an athlete got injured or pulled a muscle. It was called "Cremagesic," and it was like Icy Hot and Ben Gay mixed together, so once you rub it in it starts a heat reaction that goes into the skin.

The next day in English class when the teacher went out for his smoke break, the kids were being so nice to me and started talking about the new hair grease one of them was using from her grandmother and how well it worked. Overhearing the conversation, I was very interested and asked where I could buy some. Bonnie Ring told me that they had it at the local beauty supply store. When I told Bonnie that I'd ask my mother to get me some, she said that I could have hers since we were cool. I did not know the jar had been emptied out, and that the kids had put the therapy cream in there instead. Just as I started to put the jar of so-called grease in my purse, Bonnie asked me how I would know whether or not I'd like it if I hadn't tried it. I told her that my mother would need to look at it before I put anything on my hair, but she told me to give the jar back to her. She told me to read the jar for myself and showed me that the ingredients listed on the jar were herbs and spices, and that it was all natural. I still didn't want to use it so the girl acted as if she was putting some into her hands and rubbing it into the back of my hair. Since it looked okay to me, I took a small amount and put it onto my hair.

Bonnie told me that I needed more than I'd used because I had no edges. So, I did what she said, but when I smelled it, I became concerned. When I told her that it smelled weird, Bonnie told me that it was the herbs, but since I was rocking a Jheri Curl, I wouldn't know anything about that. I believed her and put the so-called grease on the sides of my hair and began to rub it in. Immediately it got hot and started to burn. I cried out that it was burning, and in response to my cries, the entire class broke out in laughter. Above all of the giggles and laughs, Bonnie's annoying cackle grated my nerves. It was the most irritating sound that I've ever heard, I can still remember the nightmarish sounds of her devious chuckle. I ran out of the classroom to the restroom and immediately tried to rinse my hair out in the sink, but the school sinks were too small for me to fit my head under the faucet. In desperation, I went into the bathroom stall and stuck my head into the toilet bowl. I was so upset that I cried, and cried, and cried. I had been made a fool of because I'd trusted my classmates, and my hair was ruined.

My cries must have been heard from the hallway because Robin, one of the girls who I knew from the private school, ran in and asked if I was okay. I asked her why she even cared to ask and assumed that she was in there with me just so that she could go and tell everyone that she'd found me with my head in the toilet. I begged her to just leave me alone. Robin saw how hurt I was and that I was speaking the truth. She'd never realized how badly the cruel jokes had made me feel and she promised that she would not tell anyone what had happened in the bathroom. Robin actually told me that she was sorry for the times that she had been cruel to me. She gave me a hug and I cried like a baby. We sat on the floor together and I cried and cried some more. She allowed me to get all of my tears out before returning to class. Again, I begged her not to say one word and to just leave what had happened between the two of us. She thought she owed me at least that much. Robin respected my wishes and she never told anyone what happened.

I went back to class with my hair dry as a bone, and my eyes as red as a red marker, but I didn't say a word. When the teacher asked me what had happened, I apologized to him for leaving and explained that I'd gotten sick and since he wasn't there, I'd excused myself. I insisted that I was okay. As I returned to my seat, I could hear the snickering of my classmates laughing under their breath. I just sat and zoned out. After being quiet for the rest of the day, I cried all the way home from school.

Once my parents came from work, they asked the same old question about how my day was. As usual, I told them that it was fine. However, on this day my mother asked me what was wrong with my head. I told her I was not feeling too fresh when I came home from school and that I'd taken a shower but forgot to put on my shower cap, so my hair got wet. I then asked my mother to start buying me some deodorant. Knowing that I was becoming a young lady who may need it, my mother agreed and asked no further questions. Again, the kids at school found out that they still could not break me, in spite of their cruel prank. Even still, they continued to joke on me until we finally came to the end of my sophomore year.

As a junior in high school, I was still not allowed to talk to boys or have a boyfriend. I stayed focused on sports and tried to get my father's attention. The more I looked for his blessing or his approval on how I played, the worse I felt. Nothing was ever good enough because he would compare me to other kids. *"Why can't you run like Melody Marriott? Why can't you do the high jump like Jamie Plaque? How come you can't jump the hurdles like Keyona Bling?"*

This was not what I wanted from him. I wanted my father to focus on what I was doing right, not what I was doing wrong. When I spoke up to him about how he was making me feel, he took it the wrong way and made it about himself. He told me, if I didn't like him telling me how I could do better and be better, that he just wouldn't come anymore, and that was fine with me.

One day, my new basketball coach noticed how I struggled with my right hand. When Coach Connie asked me to try using my left hand it was amazing how much of a better shooter and dribbler I was with my left hand. Combined with my height, I became a triple threat. I was scoring more points, and I was so happy. I asked my father to come to one of my games so that he could see the change for himself. I thought that now, because I was playing more and even got to play on the varsity team, he would be proud of me. He was not. After the game he asked the coach who told her to teach his child to play as a left-handed player. He went on to say that I was born right-handed, and that I write with my right hand, so why in the world would she have me playing with my left hand?

Coach Connie explained how much better I played with my left hand. She said that I could go to college with a scholarship for being a left-handed player, and that I was still able to use my right hand; I was an ambidextrous player. He heard the coach and thanked her for what she told him, but he was being phony. Once we were home, he told me that unless I went back to using my right hand, he would not come to any more of my games. He went on to say that he didn't raise a left-handed child, but a right-handed child and that is how I should be playing ball. I was stubborn, just like my father, so I calmly told him not to come. I wanted to go to college and had decided that I would do so playing with my left hand. From that day forward, I stopped using my right hand all together when it came to sports, and he stopped attending my games. In the long run it handicapped me, but in my eyes, what mattered was that I had taken a stance. What I needed to learn was the difference between hearing and truly listening to someone, but that lesson would come in due time.

I was still trying to get my mind off everything that was going on around me by getting more involved in extracurricular activities. I became a halftime dancer for the football games. I still loved to sing at church, but dance opened up a whole new avenue. I was good at it and everyone saw it. My gym coach taught a modern dance class and I blew away the entire class. Even though I was not able to see my gifts or the skills that I had, others used them against me. Instead of supporting me in my talent, they laughed at me and mocked me. I believed their criticism and allowed them to tear down my self-esteem bit by bit.

Every girl has two big events that she dreams of, that's her prom and her wedding. I never thought I would go to prom given how badly the kids at school treated me, but once again my mother worked with people who always thought well of me. My mother had a coworker who wanted her son to escort me to prom. My date was the star football player for my high school's archrival team, and I was so happy that I would be going. Waler Chance, one of the boys at my school, had even made a remark about the ugliest people who would be at prom. He had me at the top of the list, but I stood up and told him I'd bet money that I would *not* be. They had no idea who I was going with. I even told him that the girls they saw showing everything on an everyday basis will look the same. I, on the other hand, was going to take their breath away. We bet $50.00 and he continued to laugh in my face saying, my dress was going to be ruined with Jheri Curl juice running all over it. I knew that my mother was making an appointment for me to get a new curl, but I begged her to let me have a perm instead. My mother called my hairdresser to confirm that it would be okay for me to get a perm. I was feeling better about myself knowing this information. My mother even agreed to let me wear contact lenses instead of my glasses.

As I was making the transformation into a young woman, I went to find the dress that every young woman dreams of. At the dress shop I tried on so many different dresses that the people who owned the store told me that I should consider being a model for them. I felt like a princess, but I still wanted my father's thoughts on what I should wear. Before leaving, I noticed that the dress shop had a contest to win a free prom dress. I put my name in the box to enter the drawing and left thinking nothing else of it. After spending days getting ready for the upcoming prom, I got the news that my father had been laid off. With him out of work, prom would not come for me.

I went to the Lord in prayer to ask for things to turn around, and that prayer would come to pass. I received a phone call from the dress shop telling me that I had won the drawing for the free prom dress. I didn't believe the person on the phone, so I hung up on them and told my mother that people were playing on the phone. Luckily, they called back and my mother answered the phone. She assured me that it was not a joke and that I could go and pick out any dress that I wanted. As always, I was looking for my father's attention, so I invited him to come so that he could give the say-so over my dress. That year, dresses with a high slit was *the* popular style. My father picked out a multi-colored dress with a regal look. It had a queen's collar and an open back. He said this would be breathtaking and that no one would have it. All the other girls would look the same, and I should be unique. After I picked that gown, my mother found the shoes and jewelry to match. I knew that I was going to be beautiful. Even though my mother wasn't thrilled that I chose the dress that my father picked because she thought it was not as cute as the one that she picked, since I was happy, she went along with it.

The day of prom, I went to get my hair styled and found out that I was going bald in the back of my head. I started to cry and told my mother to call my date to cancel. I cried to my mother, telling her that she didn't even think that my dress was cute and now that was going bald, it was the worst day of my life. My stylist assured me that it wasn't the end of the world and that he could hide the bald spot by making a French roll to the side. It was then that my mother told me that she had only been teasing about the dress, and that she thought that it was beautiful. She went on to say that it would be even more gorgeous with the shoes and accessories, and that I would be stunning. My mother spoke the truth. I got my nails and make up done, and I was flawless. Once everything came together, I was breathtaking.

I arrived at the prom with my date, Ted Miller, everyone knew him because of his reputation as a star football player. When I turned around everyone saw that Ted was there with me and the look on their faces was priceless! I didn't even need to cash in on the $50 bet, which I knew without any doubt I'd won. I told the boy that the look on his face was all that I needed, and I walked away. I walked down the grand march and got everyone's attention. Countless pictures were being taken of me, having a one of a kind and unique dress that made it the "*Best Dress!*" Like I had said, all of the other girls looked like they did on an everyday basis. There was nothing special about them on that night. I, on the other hand, was the queen of the night, and the belle of the ball. I felt good, I was humble, and kind. I took my compliments well and did not let anything go to my head. That night was something I would cherish forever, and before I laid my head to rest, I thanked God for every moment of it.

Sadly, that joy was short-lived. A whole other storm came to pass as my hair began falling out every night on my pillow, as a result of the perm. My mother took me to her stylist who told me that she had to cut all of my hair off into a Caesar haircut. I bawled my eyes out and begged my mother to pull me out of school.

My mother did not understand where all my tears were coming from, and I did not open up to her about the abuse I'd experienced for years and was still receiving from other students. My older brother had just come back from the south where females were rocking short haircuts like boys. He said that I had the face for it. Even though he said that I would be pretty with a short "boy" haircut, due to the way that the other students had torn down my self-esteem, I was not confident enough to wear it. My mother offered to buy me a cute wig and reassured me that no one would ever know, and I could wear it until my hair grew back. She found a wig similar to Toni Braxton's hairstyle in her "Making Me High" video. I looked good in it and felt good about myself. With my contact lenses and a little makeup, I felt like I could face the kids in school with no worries. I walked into the school with a new confidence, and because of how the boys were acknowledging me since I'd turned the heads of everyone at the prom, I finally felt accepted.

However, thanks to Aiesha Mohammed, a girl who was double my size with a complexion as dark as midnight, this new-found feeling was not going to last. She was rude, mean, and did not like me getting all the attention. She told the boys that my new hairdo was not my nice hair, but a wig and that her grandmother had the same one and wore it on Sundays to church. As if that wasn't bad enough, she told them that if I did not have it tied down, they'd be able to pull my wig right off my head. During lunch one boy did just that. He pulled it off and the kids tossed my wig around the entire cafeteria. I looked like Fire Marshall Bill from the show *In Living Color*. I had no wig cap under my wig. It was embarrassing and humiliating that everyone could see that my hair was growing unevenly all around my scalp. Still, I did not cry. As bad as my eyes burned, not one tear fell until I was able to get the wig back and hide in the locker room where I bawled and cried my eyes out.

Everyday someone pulled my wig off and never, not once, did I ever fight back. I cried in Study Hall where I was alone, on my walk home when no one was around, and I cried unto the Lord. The more I prayed to God, the worse it got. Aaron Broden, a drug dealer in school, came armed with a stun gun to school. Just my luck, he was in my class. Our teacher was one of this student's customers, and as a result, it was this student, the drug dealer, who had control of the class, rather than the teacher. The kid thought it would be funny to see if my wig would fall off if he shocked me with the stun gun. He sat behind me, pulled out the stun gun, and shocked me; and yes, because I had no hair to pin my wig down to, it fell off. As I shook and fell out of my seat, the entire class burst into laughter because of my reaction. This was way too much to handle, I decided to just eat in the guidance counselor's office.

Since she was a member of my home church, I was hoping that she would see my parents and say something to them, but she never uttered one thing to them. I believe that it must have been because of her requirement to maintain student counselor confidentiality, and since I'd never given permission for her to tell my parents that I ate in her office, nothing was done. So again, I stayed prayed up about my situation. God surely let me go through, but it made my faith strong. Knowing, loving, and serving Him no matter what came my way, was all that I focused on to get me through.

By football season my hair had finally grown back, but I still did not feel comfortable wearing the boy-style haircut. I got smart and wore a hat over my wig so that if they tried to pull it off, they would grab the hat instead. After traveling back from a football game, I was gathering equipment from the bus that me and the halftime dancers had been on. One of the football players pulled my hat and my wig off. He dropped my hat, so I hurried up and put it on as my wig was being tossed around. They quickly passed it around then dropped it on the floor and stomped all over it. When I found my wig, I picked it up and put it back on, even as damaged as it was. I entered the back of the bus where no one could see me, and I cried.

As Coach Veronica Billups was doing the headcount, she asked where I was. One of the students, referring to me as *Twig*, told the coach that I was in the back of the bus crying. The coach responded by asking what the name was the student called me. She then explained to her that Twig was my nickname, and that I even knew that's what they called me. Amused with herself she chuckled after saying it. The coach walked to the back of the bus, sat down next to me, and asked if I was okay. As I wiped the tears from my eyes, I told Coach Veronica that I was okay, but asked her to promise that she would not tell my parents. She agreed to not say anything. That night when the bus arrived at the school, she walked me back to the car where my mother was waiting and as promised, she said nothing. I was quiet and spoke not one word on the ride home. My mother just thought that I was tired from the bus ride, when we arrived at home, I went straight to bed and cried myself to sleep ever so quietly.

I knew my mother's breakfast routine down pat. Monday through Friday, it was grits, eggs, sausage, toast, milk, and juice. On Saturday, it was a bowl of cereal while I watched Saturday morning cartoons, and on Sunday it was pancakes. However, this Saturday morning, I woke up to the smell of pancakes and bacon. As I entered the kitchen, both of my parents were there. I sat down confused not knowing what was to come. My mother fixed me a plate and asked me if something was wrong because I had not talked about the game the night before. I told them that there was nothing to talk about, we won like always and there was nothing special about that, and I was just tired that's all.

Suddenly, my mother shared that she'd received a phone call from my coach telling her what happened. I slammed the glass of milk that I was drinking as I thought about how the coach played me. She kept her promise to not speak to my parents that night, but she had not made a promise about the next morning. My mother asked how long this had been going on. As I looked up with a pool of tears streaming down my face, I told them that it had been going on ever since I could remember, ever since I started school. I confessed that it had been going on from the first day I realized I was different, not pretty like the other girls in my class, and even more now since they had put me in that hellhole of a school. So much more since I'd lost my hair and they'd bought me that stupid wig. Finally, all the pain, all the hurt, and all the anger finally came out as I mumbled, "Why me?"

My mother grabbed me and said that she didn't have ugly kids, that me and my brother were not ugly. Her words made the situation about her and not about me. My father even spoke to me about himself as if that was going to heal my pain. He asked me to look at him because he had been burned and had to wear a toupee. I responded with disgust because he was so off base. As a boy he was supposed to lose his hair. I am a girl, he had no idea what I went through every day.

To reassure me, my father told me that he loved me, my brother, and my mother, and that he'd protect me from this. Unfortunately, that did nothing for me, because his actions never added up to love in my eyes. My mother said that we'd need to finish up with breakfast so that we could go shopping for a new wig. She had a chance to look at my old one and could tell that it'd been through the wringer. I wiped my bloodshot eyes and told her that would be fine with me. I went to church the next day and rejoiced because I felt as if a burden had been lifted off me. I was finally able to be a child. I was able to let go of my worries and give them to my parents.

At school, on Monday after the morning announcements, I was paged over the PA system to report to the Principal's Office. I had no idea why I was being summoned, as the other students oohed and aahed, I walked out of the classroom. When I walked into the waiting area, the secretary told me to go in because they were waiting for me. I was stunned as I opened the door to the Principal's Office to see my father talking very sternly saying, "I bring my child here to get a good education, not to be picked on and harassed by these kids who have no home training. Now if one more kid puts their hands on my daughter or utters one word to her that makes her feel less than perfect, I will sue this entire school! I want my child protected when I leave her in your hands!"

I immediately ran into my father's arms, crying tears of joy as the light went off in my little head, replaying the message my mother would say to me and my brother about how much our father loved us. Now, I finally got it! My father did love me, and even though my parents had problems, which did not concern me and my brother, he cared, loved us, and would protect his family with every fiber of his being.

The principal got on the PA system, called a list of names, and instructed those kids to report to his office ASAP. Once there, he told all those who had picked on me that they were to stop immediately. He instructed the teachers to send any student to his office if they noticed them saying or doing anything to me. They would be expelled from school and would be leaving the school by police escort to their parents or guardian's home, telling them that their child will be going to jail or into the juvenile system for harassment. As soon as I returned to the class, I heard comments under students' breath calling me a tattle teller. I didn't even care because finally, after feeling so alone, I knew that my family had my back.

When football season came to an end and basketball season began, I was at last confident enough to rock a short cut with a texturizer. I was looking like the lead singer from the 90's R&B group Total. I was never told how cute the short haircut was, the boys named me "Prime Time" and Deion Sanders. I could never get a break. Every time I would score a basket, the kids would chant "PRIME TIME, NOW DO YOUR DANCE!"

I was becoming a better athlete, growing into myself and was being called a "Doable Chick" by the boys in the school. I was still a virgin but was now sneaking around trying to have a boyfriend in school, because my parents still did not allow me to date or receive calls from boys. In basketball, I played the position of center/power forward and I'd hang out at the playground just to be around boys. I would practice with them and once some of the boys saw how cool I really was and how funny I could be, they started to help me and teach me things to improve my game. I was very fond of a particular young boy who was really cute. We would hook up after practice and sit in the bleachers at school and talk and pass notes between classes.

This young man was in the gang they had made up in my town and I was cool with the boys. They would joke on me but by this time, I would joke back instead of just taking their jokes. Plus, their teasing was truly done in fun, they were not malicious. I got involved in an after-school cooking class my "boyfriend" would hang out at. His name was Dan Bundy.

I'd learned to lie at an early age, and I was good at it. I guess I'd learned it from home since my father would constantly lie to my mother. On this day, I was supposed to be at an extended basketball practice, but instead I went to meet my boyfriend. Nobody was home except for my boyfriend and his cousin, Jax. We had something to eat and drink while we watched television. Then my boyfriend asked me if I loved him. I truly did, so I told him yes; he was my first real boyfriend. But he shocked me when he told me that if I loved him, I would prove it by having sex with him right then. I asked him if he wanted to do that now, with his cousin in the house. His cousin then chimed in saying that his mom wouldn't be home for hours and that I should go ahead and show his cousin that I was about it... we could use his room. I did love him, so I grabbed his hand and said, "Let's go."

My boyfriend smiled at his cousin and took me upstairs. I was scared because this was my first time. I was trembling in fear so much that he asked if I was okay. I told him that I was, but I wasn't. As we began to kiss, he placed me on the bed. He took off his shirt and then mine. We kissed each other on the chest, sucking hard to leave hickeys to show everyone that I was no longer a virgin. My boyfriend then kissed my breasts, not knowing how endowed I was because I was not allowed to wear revealing clothes. He saw how beautiful my body was as he removed my pants. I was in my panties and he was in his tighty-whities.

All of a sudden, I heard chuckling but when I asked him if he heard it, my boyfriend convinced me that I was imagining things. As we started to hump and grind as kids do, I heard laughter again. I knew that I heard something and this time, I made Dan stop because I was sure that someone was listening in. To try to convince me that it was all in my mind, Dan called out for his cousin to come into the room. I yanked the cover over my nearly naked body, then I heard him turn off a tape recorder and leave. I was so shocked that I started to put my clothes back on. Dan tried to stop me, but I told him that I knew that he was using me. I realized that he was going to play the recording for the kids at school. He convinced me that he had nothing to do with me being set up; it was his cousin. He even made his cousin come back to the room and swear that Dan had nothing to do with it.

He started kissing me to get me to let down my guard. He pulled down my panties and took off his tighty-whities. He put on a condom and threw my legs over my head, causing me to totally flip off the bed. Feeling clumsy and embarrassed, we laughed, then he grabbed my hand and asked if I was okay. I told him I was okay, he placed me on the bed and slowly placed my legs on his shoulders and rammed himself into me. Upon entering me, I was in so much pain that I screamed out, "OH FUCK IT HURTS!" I was not even sure if there was even any stroking or pumping, but I kicked him off of me, put on clothes and ran down the stairs into a room full of the posse from his gang. They had heard everything and were laughing like it was the most hysterical thing that they'd ever heard.

I ran home to find my mother already there. All I wanted to do was take a shower to wash away the shame that I felt. Instead, my mother insisted that I join her to watch an episode of Oprah where they were talking about teens having sex. I felt as if my mother knew that I'd just had sex. When the show was over my mother asked if I had any questions. I said, "Eww, no! That's nasty!" I was relieved when my mother allowed me to be excused.

I had a friend, Tawanda, from church who was younger, but more experienced in this area, so I called her on the phone. I made sure that I spoke in a whisper so my mother could not hear my conversation. I needed to go to the bathroom but was so scared it would hurt so I needed to have Tawanda talk me through it. As soon as I started to pee it burned and I wanted to cry. Tawanda told me that it was normal. It was like a friction burn from him being inside me and not being gentle. She told me to run some water on a towel and leave it down in the area to soothe it. The slight pain went away. When Tawanda asked me how it was, I told her that it was horrible and that I would never have sex again. I told her about what happened, and she told me that Jax was a jerk for bringing his crew over to hear and that I didn't have to do it until I was really and truly ready.

At school the next day my boyfriend met me at my locker and asked if I was coming over after school so that we could finish. I asked him if he was crazy. I told him that it hurt like hell, and that I wasn't doing that. He kept trying to pressure me into going back to finish and told me that if I didn't go, it meant that I didn't love him. I told him that I didn't love him enough to go through that, plus his cousin was a jerk. When I did not give in, he broke up with me, and just like that, I lost my so-called boyfriend, all because I was not ready. I did not understand all the fuss of going through unbearable pain for something that did not feel good, so I stuck to my word to not have sex. I was in no rush, for the time being anyway.

Finally, the time had come for student athlete appreciation night. Athletes received a letter for their letterman jackets, and trophies for their accomplishments. My parents were in attendance and when my name was called, I walked on stage to accept my awards only to hear all of the kids screaming, "PRIME TIME!" My mother wanted to take her belt to each and every child, and she even had some choice words for the parents of those ungrateful children. However, I told her to pay them no mind. It was my night and I just wanted us to enjoy it.

Slowly my hair grew back and I rocked hair extensions. I tried to keep my appearance up. I would even rock braids to keep the kids from picking on my hair. My junior year was coming to a close and I was moving onward to my senior year. Senior year would be the end of four years of hell, and I would finally be able to begin a new life in college. However, I would have to study hard to keep my grades up and do well on my SATs to get into a good school.

Little did I know, this year was not going to be hell. It was actually one that I would enjoy because of Shounette Howard, a new girl who entered my school. She was the first black girl I knew with Asian eye features and colored contacts. We clicked instantaneously, and she was popular. Shounette was even crowned Homecoming Queen. To most of the girls who had been at the school since 9th grade, this was not acceptable at all. As a newcomer, not only did she come in and change everything, but she was hated because she was pretty, smart, and she stuck up for herself. In addition to taking all the pretty girls' boyfriends, she liked me and told me that now that we were friends, no one would ever pick on me, but that I had to start speaking up for myself. She even told me that if she saw the girls putting me down that she'd kick my butt. When she asked me if I understood, I said yes, then we chuckled and hugged to seal our agreement and our brand-new friendship.

My new best friend was not impressed with the boys in our town, so we would sneak over the hill and go to the club for young people. The boys we hooked up with over there, not only loved Shounette, but me as well. Those young boys loved my personality and my sense of humor, and I could dance all night. We would just have good clean fun.

I was never allowed to spend the night at any other girls' houses. However, my mother saw that my new best friend came from a military-type of home, with two parents raising their children so my mother approved of our friendship. She trusted us but had no idea that we were driving almost 60 miles to party in a different town, and that we were having the time of our lives. I was finally getting the childhood that I'd longed for.

Once I started hanging with my new best friend, people started to see that I was pretty, funny, and fun to hang around. The boys would say I was *doable*. They tried to talk to me on the down low. It was funny to me that the same popular girls who were dating the jocks had no idea the same boys were trying to get with me. It was funny that the same girl who said that my homecoming date only wanted to be with me because he was forced to be, was having trouble keeping her own boyfriend away from me. Her own boyfriend was in my ear whispering, calling me, and coming to the playground to see me. The older guys were taking a liking to me, especially the ones who went to school with my older brother or knew of him.

I started thinking about liking boys again, but unlike the last time with the boy who broke up with me because I would not finish having sex with him, I moved past that and started harmlessly flirting with the older boys. Not knowing what I was about to be faced with, I started talking to a new guy named Kyle. I did not know his real age and I was unaware that Kyle knew my older brother. Kyle was only seeing me to get back at my brother for stealing his girlfriend. Apparently, Kyle thought sleeping with me would be the best revenge.

I started to sneak out regularly to meet Kyle. He would take me to his house where he would have his way with me. During our first encounter he was nice and gentle. He knew that it was my first time, and he treated me accordingly. After that however, he regularly beat up my innocence and then threw me out of his house after he was done with me. It was always so quick, maybe all of 5 minutes, and afterwards he would kick me out and I'd quietly go home. I never told anyone, not even my experienced friend or my new best friend, Shounette. I felt dirty, as if the way that Kyle treated me was all my fault. This awakened something in me and I began to think like a boy. I wanted to be better at their game than they were. Far from being the doable chick, I now made a list of all the boys who I had my eyes on and I knew that they wanted me in return. My technique was to not give it to them on their timeline, but on my own. I was good at playing this game because I had great teachers who showed me what not to do. Both my father and my older brother left evidence of cheating all around, I then knew how to be sure to never get caught.

I went after the jocks from the basketball team, football team, volleyball team, and also the boys at the center or playground. I saw nothing wrong with getting numbers, harmless flirting, and hanging out with them at practices and playing the buddy card to be seen like I was one of the guys. My main goal was to suck in all the boys who had picked on me and to have them eating out of the palm of my hand before they realized it.

The next time I encountered sex it was with Teddie Hamler. For a change, it actually felt right, not dirty or nasty, and I was not kicked out afterwards. Instead, Teddie asked if I was hungry and if I wanted to stay after his mother got home. I knew the rule: *No Strings Attached.* So, I would leave anyway to not allow myself to get attached. It seemed like Teddie liked my grown-up mentality, so he kept me around. I started to go after older guys in my senior year of high school. I liked being pampered and being catered to. I even liked that the guys had to have me, yet I was the best kept secret. Even though the guys kept my secret and did not drag my name through the mud, I didn't know that my behavior would one day ruin my spirit.

I continued to lie to my parents, telling them that I was at whatever practice that was taking place during that season, when I was really having sex with different boys. One day when I'd really stayed after school for practice, I asked my coach for permission to stay late to use the weight room. A boy named Roy Stevens approached me and wanted to make out. I agreed and we locked ourselves in the weight room and proceeded to get ready to have sex when the janitor came in. Thankfully, the lights were off and we ran out the other door. Even though we thought we'd snuck out undetected, we had not. My coach turned me in, I was suspended, and my parents were contacted immediately. My father did not allow my mother to say a word! Even though my secret behavior was out, I'd learned to lie so well that I looked my parents in the face and told them that I was in the weight room first, and that even though the boy had come in there on his own, the janitor was lying because we weren't naked.

My father took me to school on the following day to meet with the principal. Once arriving at the school, my father walked into the Principal's Office and overheard the young man lie, saying that I had tried to force myself on him. My father got very real with him and advised Roy to tell the truth and to make sure that he neither spoke my name, nor looked my way ever again. Because of that situation, the weight room was shut down and every athlete who wanted to use the weight room had to suffer because of my choices. Having once been called *funny*, I was now known as a hoe and called *The Weight Room Girl*.

That experience scared me straight and I cut that bad behavior out very quickly. Rather than living the in-between the sheets lifestyle, I got back on the right path. I now focused on just hanging out and having good, clean fun. Having a kind of tarnished reputation, I would have to think twice about Senior Prom and who my date would be. Chance Ford, a guy who lived in a nearby town who I was very much attracted to, would be perfect. He was such a nice boy and I'd feel comfortable going with him because I knew that he'd respect my commitment to being a born-again virgin. Thankfully, he agreed to be my date.

As soon as I told people that my prom date was Chance Ford, Melody Marriott, one of the girls on the basketball team who'd made my life hell, tried to get her best friend Shonda Bateman to convince him to dump me and go with her to Prom. Thank goodness Chance was raised with morals, so he told her no and that he would still be my date. However, Melody played matchmaker and Chance and Shonda started dating and I was hurt because Chance never knew that I really liked him. Chance shared all of the details of our prom plan with Melody and Shonda, which gave them all of the information that they needed to attempt to ruin my night. Not only did he share with them our color scheme, but he also told them the tuxedo that he'd be wearing. Shonda's date got the same exact tux as Chance. Thank goodness he didn't know any of the other details that I had planned.

For my dress, I went to the same shop as the year before when I'd chosen the gorgeous multi-colored gown that my father picked. This year I selected a silver and purple dress that my mother loved. The boyish frame that I'd always been teased about came in handy when I tried on the tight-fitting dress. It was breathtaking and with my hair in an updo hair style with a swoop, it looked like the night would be perfect. Everything this year was running smoothly for me until I arrived at the grand march to see that my date and his girlfriend's date had the same tux.

I was so upset; however, my slim-framed date wore it better. Once we got to the prom, I was alone for most of the evening. Because Shonda was dating Chance, she thought that once we all arrived at the prom, they could switch dates, but I was not going for that. I told Shonda that Chance was there as my date, but she danced with him during each and every song that came on. She danced so hard that she split her dress right down the back with her big old butt. Sadly, for her, for the remainder of the dance she sat at the table by herself. Even her date ended up with another girl. I finally had Chance all to myself and I danced with him all night long. We had a great time together and went out to eat later with my best friend. Finally, I told Chance that he could go be with Shonda because by then I had other plans. My best friend, Shounette and I made our way over the hill to party with guys who liked us. Not wanting to set myself up to be bitten in the butt by karma, I still stayed on the straight and narrow and remained celibate.

I now had to focus and listen to the voice that would tell me what I should and should not do. I had stopped doing things just to fit in, not realizing that I was not designed that way. Instead, I was designed to stand out. I had no idea trying to fit in would never work for me, and that it would always be in my best interest to stand alone, even though it may not feel good. All of the things that I'd learned in grade school at the Catholic School would resurface from time to time. My knowledge of right and wrong created a war in my conscience between getting revenge, or just fitting in. It was like a tug of war within my spirit, and I no longer felt peace when I would do wrong. The tears no longer cleansed my soul because I honestly knew better, because I had home training, morals, and values.

As testing was coming up for SATs, I had to get back onto the right path to make sure that I'd be able to further my education. My passion was to become a teacher who had the compassion that some of my teachers had lacked. I'd experienced teachers who acted as if they didn't see problems experienced by their students. I wanted to help students to find their voices and speak up for themselves. Out of my four years in public school, I had only one teacher, Mr. Amsterdam, willing to defend me. He even told me to stick up for myself in his class and assured me that he would have my back, and that he would not allow anything bad to happen to me. I enjoyed his class because not only did he take me to visit colleges, but he pushed me to dream of more than just a basketball scholarship. He encouraged me to look beyond athletics and reach for greatness as a great person and a great student as well.

I then started to spend time with Ricardo Welts, whose nickname was Pepa. I'd admired Pepa since freshman year. His sister, Rachel and I played ball together, so he had known me for years. In private he acted cool, but would never give me the time of day in front of his friends. Finally, when I'd started to grow into my beauty, he wanted to talk to me as the "DOABLE CHICK." He would claim he was the first one who told me that I was beautiful, but he was clueless as to my background. He was not the first guy to ever speak those words to me. He didn't know who I really was and what I was about. Spending time with him was just something to do. As quickly as he noticed me, I was over him. Even though I knew that I would be leaving for college, and it was not right to string him along, I was not able to let go of all the times in the past when he'd been kind to me in private, only to play me in public. Why not give him a taste of the broken heart that he had given to me?

Sadly, as a female, I could not play the game of lying down with different guys without being called names, or without becoming emotionally tied to that person. After spending time together, Pepa fell for me but by that point in my life, I couldn't recognize whether he was being sincere or not. Our relationship became petty. Each of us had the attitude of, *You hurt me, I'll hurt you,* and we both missed out and it became toxic for both of us.

I kept Pepa at arm's length while focusing on studying for the SATs, getting a basketball scholarship, and getting grades good enough to help me go to college. When my brother chose to stay in the workforce rather than finish college, I vowed to do what no one in my family had done. I learned to balance my school studies with my personal life in a way that did not condemn my moral fiber of who I was trying to become as I completed high school and moved on into the real world.

I began to realize that the process of being picked on had caused me to lose focus on my education. The cruel antics of the children who had no home training made it hard for me. When it was time to make the grade and get into a top-notch school, I missed the mark. On top of that, my basketball coach helped to secure scholarships for his shining stars, but he never followed through on his promise to help me get one and I did not get accepted to the school of my dreams. However, I did get accepted to take advantage of early enrollment which helped me to get into school by taking summer classes. The idea of joining the team as a walk-on who had to start off as a bench warmer did not bother me. When I finally made it to graduation, my parents and brother were proud to see that I had made it through all I had to overcome.

It was time to gain independence, discover who I am, and learn how to live my life like it is golden...

About The Author

Y.L.G.U. (Young Lad God Understands) better known as Tamara Buchanan-Martin was born and raised in Farrell, a small town in Pennsylvania. Later, she moved to Salisbury, NC. She is a black, first-time female author of her first series "Putting It All In Words." A salesperson by day in the Automotive Industry for over twenty plus years, she is now looking to be a writer for many more. She shares gut-punching truths and how to stay strong through the obstacles of life.

She has a B.A. in Psychology from Livingstone College along with her M.B.A. in Human Resource from Columbia Southern University. She is a member of Zeta Phi Beta Sorority Inc. undergraduate chapter of Sigma Chapter, Salisbury, NC. and then onward to graduate chapter of Omicron Zeta, Raleigh NC.

Tamara loves to spend time with those who truly allow her to mentor and help. She pours into young students from her alma mater to young adults in the church. For a season, she was the YACAM Director. She is a Foster Parent, giving a home filled with stable, consistent love and support to children who have suffered traumas.

She loves traveling and seeing God's marvelous creation. While making new memories along the way, she meditates, prays and learns to praise God even the more. She looks forward to new journeys and experiences that will bless her with yet more ways to live an abundant life filled with peace for her mind, body, and soul.

Keep in touch via the web:

https://www.facebook.com/Y.L.G.U.1
https://instagram.com/omarasww/
https//www.linkedin.com/tamara-martin-41998916a

PUTTING IT ALL IN WORDS

Putting It All In Words Notes:

_____

_____

_____

_____

_____

_____

_____

_____

_____

_____

_____

_____

_____

_____

_____

_____

_____

_____

_____

_____

_____

_____

_____

_____

_____

_____

_____

_____

_____

_____

_____

Putting It All In Words Notes:

Putting It All In Words Notes:

Putting It All In Words Notes:

_____

_____

_____

_____

_____

_____

_____

_____

_____

_____

_____

_____

_____

_____

_____

_____

_____

_____

_____

_____

_____

_____

_____

_____

_____

_____

_____

_____

_____

_____

Putting It All In Words Notes:

_____

_____

_____

_____

_____

_____

_____

_____

_____

_____

_____

_____

_____

_____

_____

_____

_____

_____

_____

_____

_____

_____

_____

_____

_____

_____

_____

_____

_____

_____

Putting It All In Words Notes:

_____

_____

_____

_____

_____

_____

_____

_____

_____

_____

_____

_____

_____

_____

_____

_____

_____

_____

_____

_____

_____

_____

_____

_____

_____

_____

_____

_____

Putting It All In Words Notes:

_____
_____
_____
_____
_____
_____
_____
_____
_____
_____
_____
_____
_____
_____
_____
_____
_____
_____
_____
_____
_____
_____
_____
_____
_____
_____
_____
_____
_____
_____
_____

Putting It All In Words Notes:

_____
_____
_____
_____
_____
_____
_____
_____
_____
_____
_____
_____
_____
_____
_____
_____
_____
_____
_____
_____
_____
_____
_____
_____
_____
_____
_____
_____

CPSIA information can be obtained
at www.ICGtesting.com
Printed in the USA
BVHW080108261121
622522BV00016B/615